EVA WECHSBERG

JEWISH MINIATURES
Edited by Hermann Simon

Vol. 268A EVA WECHSBERG

All **Jewish Miniatures** may also be obtained by subscription
from the publisher.

The German National Library lists this publication in the German
National Bibliography: detailed information can be accessed on the
Internet at https://portal.dnb.de/

© 2021 Hentrich & Hentrich Verlag Berlin Leipzig
Inh. Dr. Nora Pester
Haus des Buches
Gerichtsweg 28
04103 Leipzig
info@hentrichhentrich.de
http://www.hentrichhentrich.de

Translated from the German: Lindsay Jane Munro
Typesetting: Michaela Weber
Proofreading: Nechama Rothschild
Printing: Winterwork, Borsdorf

1st edition 2021
ISBN 978-3-95565-457-3

SVEN TRAUTMANN, GABRIELE GOLDFUSS,
ANDREA LORZ

EVA WECHSBERG

A CENTENARY LIFE OF A JEWISH WOMAN
FROM LEIPZIG

WITH AFTERWORDS BY
BERND-LUTZ LANGE AND EVA WECHSBERG

Front Cover: *Eva Wechsberg, 2012 © Silvia Hauptmann*

The realization of this book was supported and financed by the Office for International Affairs, City of Leipzig. It also organizes the annual Visitors' Programme for Former Jewish Leipzigers and their Descendants. The Office maintains close relations to the Jewish Community in Leipzig and to Jewish friends and partners in Israel, the USA, Britain and many other countries.

City of Leipzig
Office for International Affairs

Content

This book is dedicated to all former citizens of Leipzig who are or were victims of the Shoah or who were forced to flee from their home city due to persecution, repression or terror.

Foreword

We are so happy that we met Eva Wechsberg as part of the Visitors' Programme for Former Jewish Leipzigers and their Descendants. During a number of meetings, Eva not only told us her story but allowed us to be a part of her life. Together we laughed and we cried, building bridges all the time between the past and the present. We are grateful for Eva's trust in us and for the deep and close friendship that developed. We were so often impressed by Eva's power and her strength of will, her chutzpah and her spirit, as well as her ability to get a sense for people and situations in the blink of an eye.

Grateful for the many hours we were able to spend with Eva, during which she inspired us, encouraged us, but also moved us, and shared her memories of the horrors of the Shoah; we had the idea of writing a miniature about Eva and her life. Many famous Jewish citizens of Leipzig, among them doctors, entrepreneurs, scientists or rabbis, have already had publications dedicated to them. By writing a book about Eva's life, we also wanted to commemorate a woman whose stories have never been told before. Dr. Nora Pester, owner and publisher of the Hentrich & Hentrich publishing house, who experienced Eva at the memorial event for the 80th anniversary of the November Pogrom in Leipzig, immediately encouraged us to make this idea a reality. We would like to thank all of Eva's friends, who helped us realize this miniature by providing advice, proofreading and carrying out research. We interviewed Eva in the summer of 2019 together with Dr. Pester. It is from this interview, from personal meetings and telephone calls, recordings of talks with pupils and other sources about Eva, including her family, that this small biography was created. It shows Eva's life, which is unique and yet also stands for the life stories of many other former citizens of Leipzig. This miniature is dedicated to all those people who Leipzig lost through the Shoah. Their loss has left behind a void in our city community that can never be filled.

Eva's very personal memories clearly show how a happy childhood in Leipzig was destroyed by anti-Semitism, racial fanaticism and hate. We want to link the story of the Jewish community in Leipzig with the fate of an individual. We want to tell people about the horrors of the November Pogrom in Leipzig, the almost complete extermination of Jewish life in the city, as well as Eva's lifesaving escape to the USA. We want to show people what her new beginning was like and how she was ultimately able to think about visiting Leipzig. While telling this story, we will repeatedly allow Eva to have her say in the form of personal quotes. We

8

did not have to translate her words for the German edition, because Eva still speaks her mother tongue perfectly, peppered with the vocabulary and phrases that were typical in the time of her childhood. We are aware that this miniature presents a Leipzig perspective of Eva's life. It was important to us to describe the life of a woman who was forced to leave the city of her birth and, at 17 years of age, had to start a completely new life with her family in the USA. Eva's life is multifaceted and diverse. She is a liberal Jew and a Zionist, a native of Leipzig and an American, she does voluntary work, and she is a widow, a mother, a grandmother and a great-grandmother. But, more than anything else, she has become a special friend to us, and we are happy that, at almost 100 years of age, Eva is still with us.

Dr. Gabriele Goldfuß, Dr. Andrea Lorz and
Dr. Sven Trautmann,
May 8, 2020

Birth and family background

Eva Miriam Abelsohn came into the world on March 2, 1922. She was born in Leipzig, in the clinic of Jewish gynecologist Dr. Arthur Littauer, located on Jacobstraße. She was the first child of Käthe Abelsohn (née Pinner, born 1899 in Görlitz) and Dr. Hans Abelsohn (born in 1895 in Bernburg). Eva's mother was an only child, and her family came from the province of Poznań. Her father was the son of a cantor. He studied Medicine in Halle an der Saale, in Freiburg im Breisgau and Berlin, but had to interrupt his studies to serve as a soldier at the front in World War One. In 1919, he received his doctor title and went to Magdeburg, where he worked as an intern. It was also the year that Dr. Hans Abelsohn and Käthe Pinner got married. As Eva tells it, they had met one year before that at a party held on the birthday of the German Emperor, Wilhelm II.

Dr. Hans Abelsohn was a member of the Zionist student association, Cartel of Jewish Fraternities (KJV), of which the philosopher Martin Buber and Chaim Weizmann, the first president of Israel were also members. At the request of friends, the Abelsohns moved to Leipzig in 1921 in order, as Eva remembers, to "consolidate Zionism in the community". It is therefore no surprise that the Jewish National Movement

Nr. 825.

Leipzig, am 9. März 1922.

Vor dem unterzeichneten Standesbeamten erschien heute, der Persönlichkeit nach _____ Familienbuch _____ anerkannt,

Der Arzt, Doktor der Medizin Hans Abelsohn,

wohnhaft in Leipzig, Frankfurter Straße 5,

und zeigte an, daß von der

Käthe Abelsohn geborenen Pinner, seiner Ehefrau,

wohnhaft bei ihnen,

zu Leipzig Jakobstraße 11, in der Privatklinik des Sanitätsrats Jakob Littauer,
am _____ ten März des Jahres tausend neunhundert zwei und zwanzig, nachmittags
um _____ drei viertel _____ Uhr ein Mädchen

geboren worden sei und daß das Kind die Vornamen

Eva Miriam

erhalten habe. _____

Vorgelesen, genehmigt und unterschrieben _____

Dr. med. Hans Abelsohn

Der Standesbeamte.

In Vertretung: _____

Nr. 825
Leipzig, den 21. November 1940.
Das nebenbezeichnete Kind führt
gesetzlich den Vornamen Sara.
Der Standesbeamte
In Vertretung:
Röffner.

Der Randvermerk vom
21. November 1940 wird gelöscht,
da die zugrunde liegende Verordnung
von 17. August 1938 aufgehoben ist.
Der Vorname "Sara" ist nicht mehr
zu führen.
Den 15. März 2000
Der Standesbeamte
OPBarge

Excerpt from the birth register

11

played a considerable role in Eva's childhood, already at an early age. Looking back, she says, "Zionism was a very natural part of my upbringing. I didn't need Hitler to tell me that I didn't belong in Germany. I already knew that anyway. Unlike many of my friends, I was very aware of being a Jew."

Leipzig, the city where Eva was born, was an important center of Jewish life in 1920s Germany. The Jewish Community of Leipzig, which was established in 1847 as an officially state-recognized organization, was a so-called "Einheitsgemeinde" (literally "united community"), and it had more than 13,000 members in the middle of the 1920s. This meant that Leipzig had the sixth-largest Jewish community in Germany. Both liberal German and orthodox East-European Jews lived together in the community, although their co-existence was not always free of religious and social tensions. In the commemorative publication for the 75th anniversary of Leipzig's community synagogue, Rabbi Dr. Felix Goldmann took quite a critical view of the designation "united community". Leipzig, he said, was "not really a community in the second half of the 19th century in the sense of spiritual and Jewish togetherness" but was far more "a large collection of Jews who did not want to merge together to create unity. And not much has changed in this respect up to the present day". He concluded that

"A Leipzig community with tradition, inner cohesion and common goals does not exist. The [Jewish] community of Leipzig is still in the process of becoming." This assessment is more or less the way Eva Wechsberg remembers it.

There were 17 synagogues and praying rooms as well as a lively community life with Torah schools and associations, kosher restaurants and numerous Jewish stores. The majority of Leipzig's Jews worked or did business in the fur trade. A great number of facilities and foundations for city society emerged on the initiative of the community members. The Eitingon family, for example, financed the building of the Jewish Hospital using funds from the Eitingon Foundation. The Harmelin family set up the Marcus Harmelin Foundation in 1930, and the Ariowitsch family sponsored a home for the elderly that was inaugurated in 1931. Numerous women from the Jewish community, like the famous women's rights activist and founder of the University for Women in Leipzig, Henriette Goldschmidt; the dedicated educator and head of the Fröbel Seminar in Gießen, Hedwig Burgheim; or the first Saxonian Educational Councilor, Gertrud Herrmann; made a valuable contribution to Leipzig society life as well as an impact throughout Germany.

A childhood in Leipzig

The Abelsohn family was well-situated and lived comfortably in Frankfurter Straße 1 (now Jahnallee), not far from the district of Brühl, where many of the Jewish fur traders were located. They belonged to the upper-middle class, were German citizens and led an assimilated Jewish life. Eva's father had a dermatology practice in the same building, before he opened a new larger one in Frankfurter Straße 6. Eva's mother was a housewife, although she actually wanted to be a schoolteacher. Eva remembers her mother as "a very attractive woman". In 1930, the family moved into a bigger apartment at Gohliser Straße 15 in Leipzig's Nordvorstadt (northern suburbs). The family had a woman to do the washing, one to do the ironing, a nanny and a maid. At Christmas, the family put up a small Christmas tree in the maid's room. Later on, the racist legislation of the Nazis meant that the family was no longer allowed to employ women as home helps.

Eva's childhood was initially very carefree. Her brother Peter was born in 1930. Eva remembers that, because he was so blond and blue-eyed, people asked why – as an Aryan boy – he didn't wear the uniform of the Hitler Youth. The Abelsohn family was well integrated into Leipzig society. The close Jewish

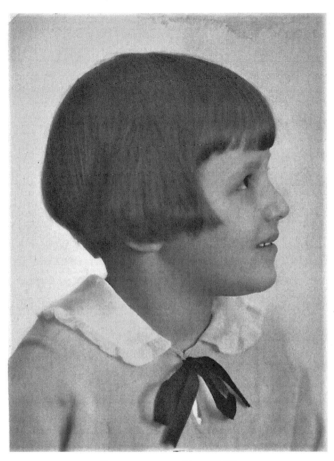

Eva as a young girl, c. 1928

and Christian friends of the family included Friedel and Albert Goldstein, the owners of the Jacoby silk store in Petersstraße; as well as the Bamberger family (owners of the department store Bamberger & Hertz) and the fur-trading family Poser. The bank directors Dr. Max Ellenbogen and Dr. Georg Kosterlitz, and numerous colleagues of Eva's father such as Dr. Richard Friedrich Bretschneider, Dr. Willy Michaelis, Dr. Nathan Körber or Dr. Raphael Chamizer were among the guests invited into the Abelsohns' apartment. The married couples Dr. Ludwig and Ilse Frankenthal and Prof. Dr. Martin and Minna Nothmann were also close friends of the Abelsohns. Their neighbors in Gohliser Straße, the large Calmanowitz family from Botosani (Romania), also quickly became friends of the family. The Abelsohns were often visited by artists from their circle of friends, and it was not unusual for them to stay overnight at the apartment. Martin Buber also visited the family. However, to Eva's great regret, when they met years later, he could no longer remember their encounter at her parent's home, despite the fact that Eva – a child at the time – had stayed up extra-late to see Buber.

Eva had a childhood like many other Jewish and non-Jewish children in Leipzig. For example, she learned to swim in Leipzig's public baths at the age of ten. Eva remembers that, at the swimming exam, each child received a small star for every quarter-hour they swam. After the exam, she had four stars on her swimming costume. Eva and her family were also members of the Leipzig Rot-Weiß e.V. tennis club and Eva also did sport at the Bar Kochba Jewish sports club. She played right-hand defense in handball, ran the 100 meters, did long jump and relay. In summer, as was usual at that time, she often played or went for walks in Leipzig's Rosental Park or went ice-skating there in winter. The family and the young Eva were particularly interested in music, theater and opera. Eva still remembers very clearly that she went to the Alte Theater in Leipzig and that admission cost 60 pfennigs. Her favorite food was "typically German": chicken fricassee with capers and the traditional meatball dish "Königsberger Klöpse".

The Abelsohn family also played an active role in religious life. Liberal in their outlook, they regularly attended the large liberal synagogue (known as "the Temple") in Gottschedstraße. The Temple was inaugurated in 1855. Eva remembers that her father "went to the religious services wearing a top hat and finely dressed. He had a small lectern in the synagogue where he kept his prayer books and other items used during the service, like his Tallit". While men and women were seated separately, there was a mixed choir. The synagogue also had a large organ. Occasionally boys from the well-known St. Thomas Choir of Leipzig sang at the services.

Unlike Eva's parents, her grandparents Lina and Samuel Abelsohn, who lived in Bernburg, had more of an orthodox orientation. According to Eva, she learned from them to "live an orthodox life without being obstinate about it." She still remembers well how she and other children learned about the Tanach, the Hebrew Bible, from Opa Samuel, and how Oma Lina always read a prayer book. As her grandfather taught the children in Yiddish, Eva learned to speak the language of East-European Judaism. Her love for her grandparents and her respect for their religious customs were what led the Abelsohns to keep a strictly kosher household.

Eva's grandmothers Lina Abelsohn and Clara Pinner both died in 1931 within only two weeks of one another – which was a terrible blow for the young Eva. Clara Pinner, whose husband Max Pinner had already died in 1927 in Görlitz, was buried in the old Jewish cemetery in Berliner Straße in Leipzig, next to her father Adolph Frank. After her Oma Lina's death, Eva's grandfather, the cantor from Bernburg, moved to Leipzig to live with Eva and her parents for a while. He died in 1938 in the Harz region.

Eva started school at the age of six and attended the Dr. Smitt'sche girls' school, a very well-known private

Golden wedding anniversary of
Eva's grandparents Lina and Samuel Abelsohn
with family and friends in Leipzig, 1928

school for girls in Jacobstraße that was shut down by
the Nazis in 1937. After that she attended Hugo Gau-
dig School in Döllnitzer Straße (today Lumumba-
straße), a mixed high school. It was there that she first
experienced anti-Semitism. Some of her fellow students said things like: "Keep your schoolbags closed,
the Jewish children steal." When the classes were di-
vided up for religious study into Jewish, Protestant
and Catholic groups, each with their own room, Eva
often heard somebody say when the lesson was over,

Eva and her grandmother Lina Abelsohn
on her 70th birthday, 1930

"Open the window, it stinks of Jews." On the day after
the Nazis seized power, a girl in Eva's class, Lilli Rosen-
berg, said to Eva: "You'll see what happens to you
dirty Jews, now that we have Hitler." At the time, Eva
received religious lessons from the rabbi and religion
teacher Dr. Hermann Ludwig, who lived in Menck-
estraße. When the anti-Semitic discrimination became
too much at her school, Eva transferred to the Jewish
high school, which was named after its founder, the
Rabbi Dr. Ephraim Carlebach. The school had origi-

nally been established for pious Jews and was mainly attended by orthodox Jews who originally came from East Europe. After 1933 however, the Jewish school was also open to liberal Jewish and German communist families and their teachers as a place of refuge. Many reform educators came to the school, meaning that Eva enjoyed both a humanist and a religious education. The form that the religious lessons took at the Carlebach School was new to Eva. Looking back at her schooltime, Eva says the following: "I was particularly good at German. I liked helping my friends with placing commas and other exercises. I didn't really like Math, and I had a friend who helped me with that." All in all, Eva looks back fondly at her time at Carlebach School. She very clearly remembers Rabbi Dr. Ephraim Carlebach and says that "he was a special kind of person." She also remembers her social-democratic and anti-fascist teacher for German, History and Mathematics, Prof. Dr. Alfred Menzel, who she still describes today as "a fantastic and progressive teacher." She remembers one sentence from her class teacher Dr. Johannes Kupfer, "there is so little that is average among the Jewish students."

Eva's carefree childhood as she generally remembers it ended on January 30, 1933 – the day that Hitler was appointed Reich Chancellor and the Nazis took power. Only a few weeks later, the ordinance by the

<u>A b s c h r i f t</u>

<u>Höhere Israelitische Schule in Leipzig</u>
(Berechtigte Realschule und Höhere Mädchenschule)

A b g a n g s - Z e u g n i s

für

Eva A b e l s o h n

Tochter des Facharztes Dr. Hans A.   in Leipzig
geboren am 2. März 1922 zu Leipzig, besuchte im Schuljahre 1937/38
die Klasse (Obersekunda) der Höheren Israelitischen Schule
zu Leipzig.
b (Sprachabtlg.)

Die Schülerin war recht gewissenhaft und strebsam; ihre Erfolge waren
befriedigend, ihr Betragen gut.

Bewertung der Einzel-Leistungen:

Hebräisch	1 = sehr gut	Geschichte	1 = sehr gut
Bibel	2 = gut	Erdkunde	2 = gut
Nachbibel.Literatur (Mischna, Gemara etc.)	———	Mathematik	3 = genügend
Jüdische Geschichte	1 = sehr gut	Physik	2 = gut
Gebete	———	Chemie	2 = gut
Religionslehre	———	Biologie	2 = gut
		Zeichnen	3 = genügend
Deutsch	2 = gut	Leibesübungen	3 = genügend
Französisch	2 = gut	Musik	1 = sehr gut
Englisch	2 = gut	Kurzschrift	———
		Latein	2 = gut

Bemerkungen: Die Schülerin hat die Reife zum Eintritt in die Oberstufe der Höheren Lehranstalten erlangt.(Obersekundareife).

Der Direktor:
gez. Dr. Weikersheimer   (Stempel)   Der Klassenlehrer:
gez. Dr. Dreifuß

Leipzig, den 1. Dezember 1937

Eva's report card from the Carlebach School

22

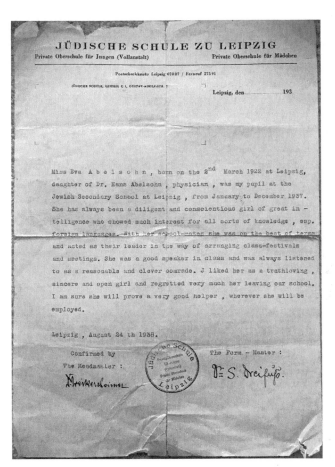

JÜDISCHE SCHULE ZU LEIPZIG

Private Oberschule für Jungen (Vollanstalt)   Private Oberschule für Mädchen

Postscheckkonto Leipzig 67007 / Fernruf 27591

JÜDISCHE SCHULE, LEIPZIG C 1, GUSTAV-ADOLF-STR. 7

Leipzig, den _____ 193_

Miss Eva A b e l s o h n , born on the 2nd March 1922 at Leipzig,
daughter of Dr. Hans Abelsohn , physician , was my pupil at the
Jewish Secondary School at Leipzig , from January to December 1937.
She has always been a diligent and conscientious girl of great in -
telligence who showed much interest for all sorts of knowledge , esp.
foreign languages. With her school-mates she was on the best of terms
and acted as their leader in the way of arranging class-festivals
and meetings. She was a good speaker in class and was always listened
to as a reasonable and clever comrade. J liked her as a truthloving ,
sincere and open girl and regretted very much her leaving our school.
I am sure she will prove a very good helper , wherever she will be
employed.

Leipzig , August 24 th 1938.

Confirmed by   The Form - Master :
The Headmaster :

Merkelscheimer   *Dr S. Dreifuß.*

Letter of recommendation for Eva from the Carlebach School

Reich President to "protect the people and the state" and the so-called "Ermächtigungsgesetz" (the Enabling Act) stripped citizens of important basic rights. A radical change to the values applied in all areas of civil life took place. This was not only apparent, but especially clear in ongoing anti-Jewish legislation and in the extensive measures to ostracize the Jewish population.

From April 1 to 3, 1933, there was already a Germany-wide boycott of Jewish stores, doctors' practices, lawyers' offices and other facilities organized by the NSDAP (National-Socialist Workers' Party of Germany) and the Reich Propaganda Ministry. April 7 saw the adoption of the Law for the Restoration of the Professional Civil Service with its so-called "Aryan paragraphs". According to these, Jews could no longer work as civil servants, unless they already had civil servant status before 1914. In April 1933, legal sanctions against Jewish doctors also came into force, which became even stricter in 1935 and prohibited them from treating non-Jewish patients. In September 1935, laws known as the "Nuremberg Race Laws" were passed. They differentiated between state citizens and Reich citizens. Only those who had "German or related blood" could be Reich citizens. They also defined the terms "Jew" and "mixed marriage". From then on, "mixed marriages" as well as extramarital relations between "Aryans" and Jews were forbidden, and these were vilified as "racial defilement" by Nazi propaganda. Jewish citizens who did not have "typically Jewish" first names also had to take on the middle name "Sara" or "Israel" from August 1938.

Anti-Semitic attacks also soon happened in Leipzig, as well as boycotts of Jewish businesses, doctors and other professional groups, and attempts to exclude Jews from public life. The everyday lives of Jewish people in the city were marked by bans and discrimination. They were not permitted to use parks or swimming pools, had to leave their schools or were prohibited from exercising their occupation or profession.

The Abelsohn family initially tried to live life as normal after 1933. Eva's father continued to work as a doctor, but he could only treat Jewish patients after 1935. Eva's mother took care of the household. The family went on holiday, traveling to the North-Sea island of Norderney, to Italy or Switzerland, until this was also forbidden by the Nazis' anti-Semitic policies. Eva surmises with a small smile that "Despite Hitler, and despite all the difficulties, my adolescent years were good."

In addition to working as a doctor, Eva's father, a staunch Zionist, was also active in the community. He was a member of the Jewish B'nai B'rith lodge and

The Abelsohn family on their winter holiday,
location unknown, c. 1935

a member of the board of the Zionist Association of
Germany/Leipzig Section. He also served as the only
Zionist community representative of Leipzig's Jewish
Community. However, from 1935 onwards, he invest-
ed most of his energy in his work on the board of
the Jewish Cultural Association (Jüdischer Kultur-
bund) in Leipzig. He became its chairman in 1936,
as the Nazis had forced his predecessor, Dr. Conrad

Goldschmidt, to be replaced. In times of increasing repressions and ostracization, the Jewish Cultural Association, which had more than 1,000 members in Leipzig in 1935, was committed to humanist values and Jewish cultural life. As such, the work of the Cultural Association was forcibly limited to the Jewish community. All events had to be registered in detail and were monitored by the police or the Gestapo (the state secret police). Despite such measures, the members of the Cultural Association, and not least the chairman Dr. Hans Abelsohn, succeeded in keeping Jewish cultural life alive in Leipzig. The association organized numerous cultural events at the Battenberg Theater in Tauchaer Straße, which had been closed in 1932 and then rented by the Jewish community from 1935. Until the work of the association was ultimately banned in 1938, the theater was used a great deal for all sorts of cultural activities, and it was the location of splendid operas, concerts and visiting revue shows by Jewish artists who only had very few opportunities to perform anymore.

Like her father, Eva was also a convinced Zionist. She wanted to emigrate to Palestine and was already registered at the Hebrew University in Jerusalem with Prof. Dr. Ernst Simon. She was a member of the Makkabi Hazair girl scout group in Leipzig, whose blue shirts were banned by the Nazis, meaning Eva had to wear a green shirt from then on. Eva took part in the meetings of the Zionist youth groups every Sabbath, going on many day trips with them. The aim of these meetings, among other things, was to prepare children and young people for emigration to Eretz Israel. It was for this purpose that she also received private lessons on modern Hebrew (Ivrit), as well as sewing machine lessons with Walter Hinrichsen, the son of the famous Leipzig music publisher and benefactor Henri Hinrichsen. "On a Singer sewing machine," she still emphasizes many years later. Her participation in these courses is worth mentioning. Only a few years before, the daughters of the upper-middle class like Eva and especially the sons of affluent entrepreneurs like Henri Hinrichsen would never have attended such a course. However, due to the increasing ostracization of Jews and because of fears about an uncertain future, many parents decided to make sure their children learned skills that could be useful when they fled or had to make a new start in life. This is also the reason why Eva did a cooking course and learned Spanish at the Berlitz School.

And even in those difficult times, it was love that made life worth living. Eva's first love was Alexander Scheiner, who everyone just called Alex, the son of an orthodox fur trader who originally came from Russia. Eva laughs when she thinks back to her parents' reaction: "My parents' biggest worry was that I might become orthodox. Eva also drew the attention of other young men. In 1937, when a team from Petach-Tikva in Palestine was visiting the Jewish Bar Kochba sports club in Leipzig, which had been established in 1920, Eva received a special proposal. One of the young men raved about his orange plantation and his own horses in Palestine. "If it was up to him, he would have taken me with him. I was very impressed, but in the end, I couldn't be persuaded to go with him to Eretz Israel," she remembers.

Eva (top, second from left)
on the playing fields of Bar Kochba
with the team from Palestine, 1937

In 1935, Eva's parents went on an "exploratory tour" with the Poser family to Palestine to check whether they could emigrate there. It was mainly Eva's mother who rejected the idea of emigrating because of the living conditions and the climate there. The couples returned to Leipzig and Eva wrote the following in her diary: "Heute ist ein großes Glück, meine Eltern kommen aus Palästina zurück." (Today is a very happy day, my parents are returning from Palestine.) At that time, Eva did not yet know how dramatic the situation in her home country was soon to become.

Despite the disappointing trip to Palestine, Eva's parents still had plans to leave Germany, where the living conditions of the Jewish population were worsening all the time. To improve Eva's English-language skills, her parents sent her for several months to an English Institute in Prague, where she completed a course and received a certificate from the German University. She arrived in Prague on March 15, 1938. It was the day on which Hitler announced the so-called "Annexation of Austria" to the German Reich on Heldenplatz in Vienna. A historical date that Eva will never forget. Eva was the only Jew at the language institute, and she encountered many anti-Semitic Sudeten Germans there. She heard other girls singing: "Und wenn das Judenblut vom Messer spritzt, dann geht's dem Nazi gut." (When Jewish blood spurts from the knife, things are good for Nazis). In 1938, it was clear to the Abelsohn family that they would have to leave Germany. Eva's father managed to flee to Rotterdam via Prague, thus escaping the developments in Germany. On October 1, 1938, Dr. Hans Abelsohn boarded the "Westerbound Voyage – T. T. S. Statendam", traveling to New York via France and England. He was able to leave Germany thanks to an affidavit, a kind of certified guarantee. He had received the affidavit thanks to a stroke of good luck, as the family did not have any family or close friends in the USA at that time. Eva still speaks full of gratitude today when she describing how her father's escape came about: "My parents remembered that, whenever it was the Jewish New Year Rosh Hashanah, my grandfather, when he was still a cantor in Bernburg, always received a check from the Freie Bank in Danzig. The check was always for five dollars and came from an Abe Cohn of 7736 Colfax Avenue, Chicago, Illinois. My grandfather never tried to find out where the check came from or why he even received it. My Papi wrote to Abe Cohn, who was a modest and very kind gentleman's outfitter. It turned out that both Abe Cohn and my grandfather originally came from Lithuania, and they were distant relatives. That was why Abe Cohn was willing to give my father an affidavit. My father then used his long-standing friendship with an employee of the

American Consulate to travel to the USA with this affidavit and to rescue the family."

However, only very few Jews managed to rescue themselves by fleeing abroad from Leipzig. Many had already fallen victim in October 1938 to the so-called "Polish Action". The Nazis deported around 5,000 remaining Jews who had Polish nationality from Leipzig to the Polish border. A few of the deported were allowed to enter Polish territory, but many others camped for several days on German-Polish no man's land. Around 1,300 people who were supposed to be deported found refuge in the Polish General Consulate in Leipzig, in the Villa Ury in Wächterstraße. On the day on which the Polish Action took place, Eva's mother was in Berlin to organize the exit visa and make the travel arrangements to get to the USA. Like many other episodes from this dramatic period, Eva can remember the events of that day exactly: "I was 16 at the time and alone at home. The telephone rang and I answered. I was told that ten Jews had jumped from the train and needed somewhere to stay. I got all of our bedding out, made the beds and laid mattresses on the floor. They stayed hiding out at our place for a few days."

Eva (right) in Prague with a young woman
she met at the language institute,
1938

The Night of the November Pogrom in Leipzig

An incident that had far-reaching consequences for Eva's life was the night of the November Pogrom from November 9 to 10 in 1938, when Germany transported people to concentration camps, burned synagogues and Jewish businesses and laid waste to Jewish people's homes. The events of November 10 in particular are etched indelibly into Eva's memory. "In the night of November 9, we heard that something was going on. I went to lessons in the morning as usual. The tram no. 24, which I always took, had to take a detour and when it stopped and I got out, I was standing in front of my synagogue – only it wasn't there anymore. It was pretty cold. I balled my fists in the pockets of my dark-blue coat from the Bamberger & Hertz department store. All I could think of was my father's prayer stool where he kept his prayer shawl (Tallit), his Bible and his prayer book, which he had used for so many years. I began looking for a telephone and called home. My little brother answered the phone, and that's when I knew the Jewish school had closed. I ran home as fast as I could. On the way, in Gohliser Straße, I saw SA men beating up some orthodox Jews, who were wearing their kaftans and large hats, on the steps down to the River Parthe."

At that point Jews were already forbidden from withdrawing money from their bank accounts. However, Eva's mother had 2,000 Marks hidden in the apartment, but Jews were not permitted to be in possession of such large sums of money. Worried that the apartment might be searched, Käthe Abelsohn and her children Eva and Peter thought about where they could conceal the money. After pondering over possible hiding places, Eva had a brilliant idea. The money was hidden in the cistern in the bathroom. It was

The burnt-out synagogue
immediately after the November Pogrom 1938 and
shortly before the ruins were pulled down

never discovered, and it helped them to prepare their escape.

At lunchtime on November 10, Eva's mother went to the police station. She wanted to deregister her husband at the authorities and inform them that he had left the country, which she hadn't done when Dr. Hans Abelsohn escaped to the USA. When Eva and her brother were at home alone one day, "three men came to the door in civilian clothing. They asked us 'Where is Dr. Abelsohn?' I said, 'Show me your ID!' and they said that that wouldn't be necessary. They then marched into the apartment and searched all the rooms. One of them sat down and put his feet up on my father's desk. They wanted to take him away, but luckily he wasn't there anymore. I said to the men that my father now lived in the USA, and they demanded proof. I showed them a letter to prove that Papi was in the USA. That wasn't enough and they wanted to see the envelope. I couldn't find it and they gave up and left. We were incredibly lucky that the men only looked around but didn't destroy anything and didn't do anything. I held my brother Peter firmly by the hand the entire time. He was only eight at the time. On the other side of the road, we could hear windowpanes being smashed, and furniture and crockery flew onto the street. It was terrible. We stood behind the curtains for three days, hardly daring to go out, and we didn't know what was going to happen next. Gestapo men in long dark-blue coats constantly entered buildings, coming out again with Jews who were then taken to the concentration camps."

Eva's father was saved from having to face all those terrors as he had already escaped to the USA. Unlike Dr. Felix Cohn, who had his practice in the same corridor opposite Dr. Hans Abelsohn's. He was shot by the Gestapo there on November 10. Critically injured, he died a short time later in the police prison in Wächterstraße, where the Gestapo had taken him. Eva still remembers today that "funerals could not take place for several days after the night of the November Pogrom. My mother and I went to the funeral. As we were standing there at the graveside, a rumor spread that the Nazis were coming to arrest the Jews who had not been taken on November 10. I still remember clearly the men creeping across the cemetery to the rear exit, which thankfully was open, in order to escape." The telephone rang that evening and Eva's non-Jewish teacher from her sewing-machine course, whose name she can no longer remember, was on the other end. "She asked if she could help. We thanked her for offering but, scared for her safety, we said, 'Hang up!'" One of Eva's best non-Jewish friends up until the night of the Pogrom was Brigitte Leipold. After the Pogrom, Eva gave her friend the following warning: "Don't meet with me. It isn't good for you." After the war, Eva put an advert in the newspaper in search of her friend. Brigitte Leipold, who was then living in Munich, read it and answered. The two women remained lifelong friends after that.

Looking back, Eva describes the events of the night of the November Pogrom as follows: "No matter where I begin to tell my story, I always come back again and again to that particular day, because it was so terrible and so significant. All I can say is how happy and how grateful I am that my mother and my brother and I survived. Others did not." After the November Pogrom, the bank director and friend of the family, Dr. Georg Kosterlitz (1882–1942), was hidden by the Abelsohns in their apartment for a few days. However, he was arrested in 1938 as part of the so-called Sonderaktionen (special commandos) and deported to Sachsenhausen and then later to Buchenwald concentration camp. On November 11, 1942, he was murdered in Auschwitz.

In the ensuing weeks, the moves to exclude Jews from public life became increasingly intense. Jews were forbidden from attending cultural events and public schools, and they were also not allowed to spend time in public places or parks. In December 1938, the "forced Aryanization" of Jewish businesses and stores took place without any compensation, and

"Aryan" trustees took over. In April 1939, a law was passed pertaining to "tenancy agreements with Jews", which allowed non-Jewish landlords to evict Jewish tenants. As a result, Jewish citizens were forced to take in Jews who did not have an apartment. This paved the way for the so-called 'Juden Häuser' ('Jewish houses'), of which the first 47 were established in Leipzig in the fall of 1939.

Escape to the USA

Käthe Abelsohn and her children Eva and Peter initially spent the weeks after the horrors of the November Pogrom in Leipzig. They continued to prepare for their escape from Europe. However, according to Eva's recollection, they had to leave their apartment on Gohliser Straße and move for a short time. With the help of a former patient of Dr. Hans Abelsohn, Mr. Engelke, who was the head of the foreign exchange office, Eva's mother Käthe Abelsohn managed to get all the family's property as well as the medical equipment from her father's practice over to the USA. That was an absolute exception in those days. As a thank-you, Mr. Engelke was allowed to choose something from the Abelsohn family household as a gift to himself. He sent Mr. Schiller, who picked out a Grundig radio, a bust of a woman, and a record of the opera *L'Africaine* by the Jewish composer Giacomo Meyerbeer. At the same time, Eva was working for a while in the community kindergarten. When she complained of abdominal pain one day, her mother took the precaution of having her appendix removed at the Jewish Eitingon Hospital, which had been run for many years by Dr. Ludwig Frankenthal, and where Dr. Manfred Bergmann was the last remaining doctor after the November Pogrom. She was worried that her daughter could suffer a ruptured appendix and that no medical help would be available during the planned escape. In the hospital, Eva saw traumatized people with serious injuries who had returned from the concentration camps after their initial internment.

After anxious weeks, Käthe Abelsohn succeeded in obtaining a US visa for herself and the children to ensure that the family could be reunited. The visa reached the family on March 2, Eva's birthday. On March 21, 1939, the three were finally able to follow their father by train to Hamburg and then by ship to the United States. The three had 10 Reichsmarks each on them, the maximum amount of money that Jews were allowed to carry when they left the country.

Immediately after arriving in New York, the family headed to Chicago, where they were met and welcomed at the station by Abe and Anni Cohn, the guarantors of the affidavit. In 1940, the Nazis withdrew the family's German citizenship and Dr. Hans Abelsohn was deprived of his doctorate.

A new start and life in the USA

In Chicago, Dr. Hans Abelsohn did not find it easy to resume his work as a doctor. He had to study for a year in order to be allowed to practice medicine again and to be able to open a new practice. Since the family had no other income at that time, they sublet one of their rooms. Eva's mother went to work in West Chicago, where she baked cookies for three dollars a day, allowing her to contribute to the family's upkeep. At home, the family continued to speak German and belonged to the German-Jewish Habonim congregation in Chicago.

Through the Jewish Federation, Eva was initially employed as a maid and nanny for two years—hard work that only paid four dollars a week. She took care of the household, nursed the family's child at night, and cooked and cleaned. She then attended business school. Although her father took the view that Eva should study, she thought that there were more important things to deal with first and that she ought to earn money. The years as a maid were not an easy time for Eva, as, back in Leipzig, the Abelsohn family had had maids of their own to help around the house. In 1941, at the age of 19, Eva married her first husband, Gerhard (Gerry) Bergmann, who came from Berlin and had left Germany as early as 1934. His family had also settled in Chicago and owned several shoe stores. Eva and her first husband had met by chance, as Gerhard Bergmann's aunt worked in the pharmacy of the hospital where Dr. Hans Abelsohn was doing an internship as part of his renewed studies. Eva's husband proudly served his adopted home country during World War Two. Two years after the wedding, in 1943, Eva's first daughter Judith was born. Another daughter, Margaret, followed in 1947; she is always known as Peggy. At home, the young family spoke English.

Another defining event in Eva's life occurred on November 29, 1947, when two-thirds of the United Nations General Assembly voted in favor of a partition plan for Palestine and the establishment of a Jewish state. It was a significant moment that the dedicated Zionist had not dared to dream of. Thousands of Jews celebrated at Chicago's Soldier Field. On May 14, 1948, the State of Israel was founded. "Since that day," says Eva, "I have been certain that there is always a place of refuge where Jews can find protec-

Eva with daughter Judith, 1944

tion from persecution and discrimination. For many years I felt a great longing to move to Israel. However, I chose to stay with my family in the USA and support the State of Israel from afar."

Instead of moving to Israel, Eva, her husband, and their two daughters moved to Detroit in 1949 for work. Detroit had a large community of Shoah survivors who had immigrated to the USA after their liberation from the concentration camps. As a volunteer, Eva gave language courses and helped survivors organize their daily lives. In 1953, Eva and her family returned to Chicago, where Gerhard opened his own shoe store where Eva would also later work. After many years of marriage, Eva divorced Gerhard and got remarried in 1961. Her second husband, Rabbi Dr. Bern(h)ard Wechsberg, was born in Katowice in 1911. He attended university and the famous rabbinical seminary in Wrocław (then Breslau). He got his doctorate in 1936 and was ordained a rabbi in the same year. He was one of the last graduates of the rabbinical seminary before it was destroyed by the Nazis. In 1938, shortly before the November Pogrom, he moved to the USA and settled in California. Although Eva and Dr. Bernard Wechsberg met in Chicago, he continued to love California and always dreamed of returning there. Ultimately, the couple moved to Rancho Palos Verdes, a suburb of Los Angeles, in 1962.

Wedding picture of Eva and Dr. Bernard Wechsberg,
1961

In Rancho Palos Verdes, Dr. Bernard Wechsberg became rabbi of the Ner Tamid congregation, where he was active until he died in 1992. The congregation was still very young and was initially comprised of 18 families with many children. The Wechsberg couple was very involved in the congregation and contributed significantly to its growth to over 600 members. In 1964, Eva and her husband moved into a large, detached house with an ocean view. At that time, the congregation did not yet have its own synagogue, so the Wechsbergs' family home was always open to worshipers. Eva welcomed the children who came to receive lessons from Rabbi Wechsberg. No other address would be Eva's home longer than this one: "I love this house. They'll have to carry me out of here one day," she laughs.

Although Eva was very happy in California, she loved to travel. "After my husband retired, we often went on cruises. We got to see every continent," Eva recalls. Even on their voyages, Dr. Bernard Wechsberg worked as a rabbi and Eva acted as a special contact for other travelers. Later, in the 1980s, Eva started working as a travel agent. Considering her great passion for travel, this line of work seemed tailor-made for Eva; she worked as a travel agent for more than 35 years. Even over 90, Eva continued to work full-time in the travel agency for a long time.

In addition to her work, Eva was involved in volunteering for more than 50 years and received several awards for this. Like her father had been earlier in Leipzig, she was mainly active for Zionist institutions. From 1970 to 1972, she was Pacific South West Region president of the Women's League for Conservative Judaism, an organization that aimed to strengthen and support Jewish women's groups and raise money for an educational institute, a Torah Fund, and other projects. Eva was then National Vice President of this organization from 1972. In addition to her dedication to her community, she worked for the United Jewish Appeal, the Los Angeles Jewish Federation, and other organizations such as Hadassah. She supported the establishment of synagogues in Israel. Many times, even in her mid-90s, she continued to speak to schoolchildren and adults about her story, her family's life in Leipzig, and her escape to the USA. Eva took part in numerous commemorative and memorial services for the victims of the Shoah and supported projects through donations.

After her husband died, Eva remained alone in her house in Rancho Palos Verdes. Even today, she is convinced that widows can cope better with living alone than widowers can. "Sometimes I am happy and sometimes I am sad, but I am never alone. Only rarely do I feel lonely."

Family and friends

Eva's long life in the USA has been marked by many happy moments and some hard times. After her father retired, Eva's parents moved to California and lived in the Wechsbergs' house. In 1967, her younger brother Peter died of leukemia. He was married and left behind five children. Eva's father also died that same year. Her mother, Käthe Abelsohn, followed in 1979. Eva's two daughters were, however, a source of joy. In 1967, her daughter Judith married. In 1971, Judith's daughter Lisa was born, making Eva a grandmother for the first time. A little later, Lisa's brother Aaron was born. Judith has a Master of Arts degree and worked as a social worker in Boston. Eva's daughter Peggy was also married but was widowed at an early age. She has four children: Oren, Ethan, Tamar, and Netta. Peggy and her husband lived in Israel for 15 years before returning to the USA in 1981. There, she went back to college and received a doctorate in psychology at the age of 49. Since then, she has worked as Senior Director for Jewish Family Service. Eva has a total of six grandchildren and became a great-grandmother for the eighth time in September 2020.

Throughout their lives, the well-known biochemist Dr. Ellen Borenfreund was Eva's best friend: "Our mothers knew each other even back in Leipzig. Ellen,

Eva's daughters Judith and Peggy
with their grandparents Dr. Hans and Käthe Abelsohn,
c. 1960

49

like me, was born in Leipzig in March 1922 and our mothers pushed our prams together through Leipzig's Rosental Park. Later, Ellen and I were in the same class at school". The Borenfreund family was able to escape to the United States before the Abelsohn family. Their common background and similar experience created a deep bond between the two Leipzig-born women. Although Eva and her friends lived in different cities, they stayed in close contact, phoned each other every Saturday, and visited each other regularly.

Eva (second from right) on her 90th birthday
with her son-in-law Larry Neimark and her daughters
Judy and Peggy, 2012

One of these visits took place on November 9, 1989. It was not only the 51st anniversary of the November Pogrom but also the day Eva and her friend watched the Berlin Wall fall on television. The fact that it was another November 9 when the world changed and the fact that she spent that day with her friend from Leipzig is something that Eva comments with the words "God has a funny sense of humor!"

Eva also kept in touch with numerous other Jewish Leipzig natives who had survived the Shoah: "Many of my dear old friends from my class have emigrated to Israel, and as far as they are still alive, I am in contact with them." The same applies to former Leipzig citizens she knows in the USA. Among her most important friends from her Leipzig days were the married couple Margot and Henry (Heinz) Bamberger in the USA and Anni Taub and Herta Weiß in Israel. Alex Scheiner, Eva's childhood sweetheart, also lived in Israel. The two maintained a special, friendly connection throughout their lives. A special connection also developed with Benjamin Safran, who came from Leipzig and lived in Israel. Eva remembers: "Among the Leipzig friends I met again in Israel was my friend Benny Safran. In the 1990s, when we had both lost our spouses, our friendship developed into a very special bond. We truly became "wandering Jews" because we traveled back and forth. We spent a lot of time together in Israel and California. In Europe, Benny showed me the cities of Paris and Brussels, where he lived and worked as an enologist (wine expert) for the Israeli state. We got to know each other's children and, even after Benny's death, his children and I stay in very close touch." Eva often traveled within the USA or to Israel to meet up with old friends who lived all over the world. And in Leipzig, too, she found new friends again. In addition to the intense personal contact with the many former

Three former citizens of Leipzig:
Margot Bamberger (née Storch), Eva Wechsberg and
Raja Desenberg (née Rubinstein), 2012

Leipzig citizens around the world, it was above all the Association of Former Leipziger in Israel, founded in 1953, which allowed Eva to keep in touch with her former homeland. Although she did not live in Israel, she became a member and always eagerly awaited the association's newsletter that appeared several times a year. The newsletters kept readers informed about weddings, births and other joyful events as well as about the activities of the association.

Rapprochement with Leipzig

Since fleeing Leipzig in March 1939, Eva always felt American. She says with pride: "Being an American means the world to me. This country saved my life." Nevertheless, Eva was always interested in keeping up with what had become of the city of her birth. In the 1980s, she came to Leipzig for a short visit with her second husband. On that occasion, the two made a round trip through the GDR and visited Dresden and Meissen. They even came to Leipzig for a day and stayed at the Hotel Merkur (today called The Westin Leipzig).

At that time, the small Jewish community of less than 40 members was mostly very elderly. Jewish life in the city was barely perceptible.

Eva and the Chairwoman of the Association of Former Leipziger
in Israel, Channa Gildoni,
in the Brody Synagogue in Leipzig, 2017

After the "Peaceful Revolution" in the fall of 1989
and German reunification in 1990, new opportunities arose for Eva to visit her native city. The City
of Leipzig initiated a Visitors' Programme for Former
Jewish Leipzigers and was able to invite a group of
former city residents from Israel to Leipzig for the
first time in November 1992. Eva also got wind of the
program through friends in Israel and the USA, and
she decided in September 1993 to write a letter to the
City of Leipzig expressing her wish for an invitation.
That same month, she received a reply from Leipzig's

City President Friedrich Magirius. As the city had just started to establish the Visitor's Programme, an invitation was not possible straight away. However, sporadic correspondence developed between the city and Eva. She wrote to Dr. Hinrich Lehmann-Grube, Mayor of Leipzig: "I would be very grateful if you could let me know what my chances are. I don't want to annoy you, but I would love to show my children the city where I came from and where I spent my youth until I was 17. My grandmother and great-grandfather are buried in the old Jewish cemetery."

Visitors' Programme for Former Jewish Leipzigers and their Descendants

Leipzig's Jewish Community, known as the "Israelitische Religionsgemeinde zu Leipzig", was founded in 1847 and was the sixth-largest community in Germany with approximately 13,000 members before the Nazis seized power. The community was almost completely decimated because people fled, were displaced and were victims of the crimes and murders committed during the Shoah. The few survivors who returned to Leipzig in 1945 upheld the traditions of Jewish life in the city.

At the end of the 1980s, the first contacts took place between former citizens of Leipzig in Israel and the Jewish community of Leipzig. As a result of the "Peaceful Revolution", these connections continued to increase and intensify. Representatives of the Association of Former Leipziger in Israel and numerous individuals from all over the world approached Leipzig's city administration with their desire to once again visit the city of their birth. Aware of its historical responsibility, the City of Leipzig initiated the Visitor's Programme for former Jewish Citizens of Leipzig in 1991. The first invitation was sent round about the Memorial Day for the November Pogrom, from November 1 to 11, 1992. The City of Leipzig was

Eva (front row left), her daughter Judith (behind Eva)
and the group of former residents of Leipzig as guests of the
Mayor Burkhard Jung in the New City Hall, 2013

clear about the fact that this could only be a symbolic gesture. Adequate compensation for the suffering experienced or even restitution was not possible. The city has been inviting a group of visitors one to two times a year since 1992. Because of their age, in the 2000s an increasing number of former Leipzig citizens could not accept the city's invitation and the number of visitors to the program greatly reduced. At the same time, the interest among family members of the second and third generation in the program was increasing all the time. Because of this, the City Council decided in 2009 to open up the program to children and grandchildren. It was important to the City of Leipzig to offer descendants of former Jewish citizens the chance to remain in contact with Leipzig and to discover the place where there were both pleasant and terrible memories in the family history.

Today, the City of Leipzig invites guests every year during the week-long Visitors' Programme for Former Jewish Leipzigers and their Descendants so that they can get to know the city. They are welcomed by the Mayor of Leipzig at a reception held in the town hall. The guests explore the city and gain an insight into Jewish life in Leipzig today and in earlier times. They visit the synagogue and come together with Jewish and non-Jewish city inhabitants at different events. The program activities also include a city tour, a visit to the old and the new Jewish cemetery, as well as participation in various cultural events. Talks with school students are also a fixed part of the program. Every two years the visit is integrated into the Leipzig Jewish Week, which happens at the same time. The Visitor's programme is made possible by broad engagement from Leipzig's civil society and different sections of the city administration. It is organized by the Office for International Affairs of the City of Leipzig, and would not be possible without the work of a great number of volunteers. There is cross-party consensus in Leipzig's city council concerning the commemoration of the City of Leipzig's Jewish heritage through the Visitor's Programme and about creating new connections between the city and the descendants of former Jewish citizens of Leipzig.

At the beginning of February 1996, Eva received a letter dated January 31 from the Office for International Affairs of the City of Leipzig with an invitation to take part in the Visitor's Programme in 1996. Eva was excited about the invitation and gladly accepted it writing:
"I am particularly looking forward to the concert in the Gewandhaus, and the other plans also sound interesting." Eva had last seen the Gewandhaus in

Leipzig when she was 15 and attended the dress rehearsal of a performance of Ludwig van Beethoven's 9th Symphony. Eva and her daughter Judith landed in Leipzig on April 21. They were welcomed at the town hall by Dr. Hinrich Lehman-Grube and were allowed to enter their names on the Golden Book of the City of Leipzig. Eva and her daughter visited the graves of Eva's grandmother and her great-grandfather in the old Jewish cemetery. When she and her daughter Judith saw the graves, they were both very moved. Her daughter has the middle name Clara in memory of Eva's grandmother. When mother and daughter stood before the graves of Clara Pinner and Adolph Frank, Eva stated: "Hitler did not win." As part of the Visitor's Programme, Eva and her daughter also attended the Prayer for Peace in Nikolaikirche (Church of St. Nicholas) from where the Monday demonstrations proceeded in 1989.

As a symbol of Jewish-Christian dialog, Eva read out a prayer in Hebrew during the service. She was also received in the American General Consulate with Judith. Eva also remembers: "We were invited to a concert in the Gewandhaus. When I heard the beautiful music by Bruch and Gershwin, I thought back to my youth when Jews were not allowed to go to a concert and when it was strictly forbidden to perform music by Jewish composers." She also visited Leipzig's

Eva M. Wechsberg
28503 Trailriders Drive
Rancho Palos Verdes Ca 90274

USA

7. September 1993

Rat der Stadt Leipzig
Burgplatz 1
0-7010 Leipzig
Deutschland

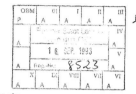

Sehr geehrte Herren,   1081   16. 9. 93

seit vielen Jahren hatte ich gehofft, nach Leipzig engeladen zu

werden, aber so lange Deutschland geteilt war, war das natuerlich

nicht moeglich.

Nun ist das doch Alles anders geworden,und ich waere Ihnen sehr dankbar,

eine Einladung zu erhalten.

Ich bin am 2 Maerz 1922 in Leipzig geboren, bin die Tochter von Dr. Hans

und Kaethe Abelsohn und habe bis zum 21. Maerz 1939 in Leipzig gelebt.

Meine Grossmutter and mein Urgrossvater sind in Leipzig begraben,mein

Vater praktizierte bis 1938 in Leipzig as Dermatologe.

Es wuerde mir sehr viel bedeuten,Leipzig nach so vielen Jahren wieder

zu sehen und meiner Tochter zu zeigen, woher ich kam.

Ich hoffe, dass die Moeglichkeit besteht ine Einladung zu erhalten und

bin Ihnen schon jetzt sehr dankbar.

Mit vorzueglicher Hochachtung

Eva M. Wechsberg

Eva M. Wechsberg, geborene Abelsohn

Letter from Eva to the Leipzig city authorities, 1993

61

only synagogue that was not destroyed. The so-called "Brody Synagogue", which was inaugurated in 1904 at Keilstraße 4, already existed before Eva was born. It is integrated into a residential building, which is why, while the Nazis laid waste to the interior and threw everything they found inside onto the street, they were unable to set fire to the building. It survived the Second World War and was able to be re-established as a synagogue for religious services again in 1945.

The grave of Clara Pinner and Adolph Frank in the "Alter Israelitischer Friedhof" Jewish cemetery during her 1996 visit

After this first visit to the city of her birth, Eva wrote: "I am so grateful for your kind welcome (with beautiful roses) and for taking care of us so touchingly during the entire stay. I really did not know what to expect and I did not think that you and your colleagues would make it possible for my visit to my old home city to be such a positive one. We cannot forget, and we cannot forgive, but I am happy that I have got to know the new German generation and to experience first-hand that we can look positively to the future."

Her 1996 visit gave rise to a longing for Leipzig in Eva, and she has repeatedly visited the city since. She came back again in 1997, this time also for the Visitors' Programme for Former Jewish Leipzigers and their Descendants. It coincided with the city's second Jewish Week and the 150th anniversary of the establishment of Leipzig's Jewish community. There was a large festive religious service in the synagogue and Eva met many old friends and people she had attended school with who now lived in the USA, Israel, Latin America or Europe. She did not know before that some of them had survived the Shoah. Eva remembers: "I came with Benny to Leipzig and our joint visit to the Jewish Week was a very special thing for us. It was so meaningful and so strange all at the same time to visit the places of my childhood and to celebrate this special week and the Jewish community anniversary in Leipzig."

In the 1990s, Eva also began to apply for compensation for the material losses the family suffered in Görlitz and Berlin. She was able to get a small sum for the lost property and her father's practice. This could, of course, never compensate or even make good for the life they lost in Leipzig.

Eva visited Leipzig regularly in the years that followed, often coming especially for the Jewish Week every two years – a cultural festival dedicated to Jewish life in the past and present. As part of the Jewish Week, Eva attended concerts, readings, workshops, films, lectures, exhibitions, theater and dance performances, and she always spoke to school classes as a witness of the past. In 2013, she was once again accompanied by her daughter Judith. One year before, Eva had heard from her friend Henry Bamberger that there was to be a lecture at the Ariowitsch Haus by the Ephraim Carlebach Foundation about the Jewish Cultural Association and the work of her father Dr. Hans Abelsohn. Eva, now 90 years of age, quickly decided to buy a plane ticket, arriving at the event to the great surprise of all present.

During one of her visits to Leipzig, Eva also traveled with her friend Dr. Hubert Lang to Bernburg, where her father was born. They visited the Memorial to the

Victims of NS Euthanasia there. From 1940, one of the central "Euthanasia" facilities was located there on the premises of what is now a specialist clinic. Approximately 14,000 patients from sanatoriums and care homes as well as prisoners from the concentration camps Buchenwald, Flossenbürg, Groß-Rosen, Neuengamme, Ravensbrück and Sachsenhausen were murdered using gas in Bernburg. After viewing the memorial, they both went to the Jewish cemetery in Bernburg. To their great dismay, this had been almost completely destroyed and they were unable to find the graves of their grandparents. Eva still remembers today their visit to view the memorial and go to the cemetery: "I was so grateful that I wasn't alone that day but accompanied by my friend Hubert. I remember it as if it was yesterday. We held hands as we went from room to room in the memorial building, horrified. I was extremely sad and angry at the cemetery. It was one of the most emotional days in my life, and I will never forget it."

A visit in the summer of 2015 was especially moving for Eva. 77 years had passed since the November Pogrom, the night in which "her synagogue" had gone up in flames. A memorial had been installed at the location where the synagogue had been in 2001. It traces the outlines of the synagogue and commemorates it with 140 bronze chairs where people can sit and remember. A religious service took place on these chairs as part of the 2015 Jewish Week with community Rabbi Zsolt Balla. A great number of former Jewish citizens of Leipzig and their family members attended the service. Eva was the only person present who had actually prayed in the synagogue as a child, and she therefore embodied a special link between the past and the present.

The fact that Leipzig's Jewish community is so lively and active today gives Eva great satisfaction and she sees it as another victory over Hitler and the Nazis.

November 2018 saw Eva once again visit the city of her birth. At the invitation of Leipzig's Mayor, she was invited as an honorary guest at the commemorative event in remembrance of the crimes committed during the November Pogrom. Eva spoke on behalf of all former Jewish citizens of Leipzig exactly 80 years to the day after watching the Temple burn. She reminded them of the city's Jewish history and described in emotional images her personal experiences of November 1938. She concluded her address with the following words: "I feel as if I am almost home again." During her visit, Eva also spoke to a school class and in St. Thomas's Church about everything she had experienced. She met many friends and was invited by the Director of Leipzig Opera, Prof. Ulf Schirmer, to enjoy the performance of Rigoletto from a box at the opera house: "It was a wonderful performance and I felt very flattered when 'Rigoletto' came to meet me during the break. What a surprise!"

After spending a week in Israel, Eva returned to Leipzig again in 2019. The occasion was once again the Jewish Week and the Visitors' Programme for Former Jewish Leipzigers and their Descendants. Eva went to see the performance that had resulted from a project week in schools titled "The 1938 November Pogrom in Leipzig – A Turning Point in the Life of the Young Eva Abelsohn" at the social and cultural center WERK 2. In Eva's presence, the school students presented their own texts and performed these in different creative ways. The project took place in cooperation between the Ephraim Carlebach Foundation and the Rudolf Hildebrand School, the Rahn Education and the Henriette Goldschmidt School. Particularly impressive for Eva in 2019 was the concluding concert of the 13th Jewish Week. It took place in the East Concourse of Leipzig's main railway station and was organized by the City of Leipzig, the Ariowitsch Haus and the Leipziger Synagogalchor (Leipzig's Synagogal Choir), under the direction of Ludwig Böhme. Titled "Bloch im Bahnhof" (Bloch in the Station), more than 200 people from different choirs and orchestras from Germany and Israel performed the choir symphony *Avodath Hakodesh* by

Eva during her address in commemoration
of the November Pogrom, November 2018

Ernst Bloch. It was above all the Jewish prayers and the symbolism of the main station, which was also the first station along the Abelsohn's family escape route from Leipzig that moved Eva to tears.

Today, Eva is the oldest surviving former Jewish citizen of Leipzig. During her visits, she was able to see how Jewish life had once again developed in Leipzig. After the collapse of the Soviet Union, many Jews came to the city. The community began to grow again and now has more than 1,250 members. It is the largest community in the east of Germany and has an orthodox orientation. The community once again enjoys a lively and active community life. Services take place three times a day at the synagogue, and the community members celebrate Bar Mitzvah's, Bat Mitzvah's, weddings and the Jewish festivities together. A Torah center, family club and other interest groups provide the framework for numerous community activities. Since 2009, the Ariowitsch Haus has given the community a unique center for culture and a place to come together. A kosher restaurant, Café Salomon, once again opened in Leipzig in 2019.

During her visits to Leipzig, Eva made many new friends, who were one of the reasons why she continued to visit the city. She became especially close friends with Dr. Hubert Lang, Stefanie and Bernd-Lutz Lange, Dr. Andrea Lorz, Katja Roloff, the

Leipziger Synagogalchor under the direction of Ludwig Böhme, the Ephraim Carlebach Foundation, which was set up in 1992, and the authors of this book. Eva also shared an old recipe of her mother for "kalte Kuchchen" (literally 'cold cakes'), which she would also like to include in this book:

For the dough:
½ pound of butter (at room temperature)
½ pound of flour
½ pound cream cheese (at room temperature)

For the filling:
Split almonds
Raisins
Sugar
125g melted butter
1 egg yolk

Method:
- Mix the flour, cream cheese and butter
- Form the dough into a ball, wrap it in cling film and leave it overnight in the fridge
- Take the dough out of the fridge at least one hour before baking
- Cut the dough into 4 portions and roll each portion out on a floured surface

Eva on her 98th birthday
in the house of her daughter Peggy, 2020

- Brush surface of each portion of dough with melted butter
- Sprinkle sugar, almonds and raisins on top of the butter
- Roll all 4 portions of dough and cut about 3 cm into the dough using a sharp knife
- Brush the rolls of dough with the egg yolk
- Bake for about half an hour at 190°C (375 degree Fahrenheit) until they are golden brown
- Allow them to cool and cut them into individual serving portions

Talking about rekindling her connection to Leipzig, Eva says: "What happened cannot be forgiven. But life goes on. I am especially grateful that the City of Leipzig maintains such good relations with its former citizens. Leipzig does a great deal to welcome us survivors and now the second generation, and to express how great the human and cultural loss was and how sorry the city is for what happened."

Eva during her most recent visit to Leipzig
with Mayor Burkhard Jung
in the Old City Hall, summer 2019

Afterword by a Leipzig Friend

From Gohlis to America

Any prejudices you might have against old people — really old people who are over ninety — have to be thrown overboard when it comes to Eva Wechsberg. My memory of our first encounter in spring 1996 is that of a bright-eyed, smartly dressed, well-groomed woman who looks at you attentively and smiles kindly. What a courageous woman, I thought, who, despite her age and the visual impairment you might expect, puts herself through this grueling flight. She takes it all in her stride. Perhaps one reason she has retained her love of travel is that she used to work in the tourism industry.

In conversation, it becomes clear that she has fine antennae for light-hearted remarks and has a dry sense of humor herself. If there had been no Hitler and no Nazi dictatorship, Eva and I might have met at some point as citizens of Leipzig after a cabaret performance in the basement of the Academixer and talked about everything under the sun.

She speaks clear High German — in contrast to some German emigrants who, after decades, have an unmistakable American accent. What you soon realize is that Eva is a woman who — to use an old-fashioned expression — doesn't let herself be put over a barrel. She knows what she wants. And she has known that for quite a long time now.

Eva Wechsberg is now presumably the last Jewish woman in Leipzig to have experienced the horror of the November pogrom of 1938 as a 16-year-old girl. What must have been going through her mind on November 10 that year, standing in front of the ruins of the synagogue? How can a young person — at that time she was usually known as 'Evchen' Abelsohn, and was born and raised in Leipzig — deal with such hatred? That was simply beyond comprehension. There can only be horror at the forms of violence and fear as to how it will continue for her and her family. At that time, there was no way of knowing that she would speak in another Germany to commemorate the place where the synagogue once stood. And in another year, she impressed an audience in St. Thomas Church with her memories.

In her childhood and youth, Eva of course also had some lovely experiences in this city and so she also retains good feelings for the city of her birth. And speaking of feelings — of course one of them includes the fact that she was in love here for the first time in her life.

In conversation, it becomes clear that Eva Wechsberg was particularly friendly with another Leipzig couple once she got to the USA: Margot and Henry Bamberger. There, former residents of this city were able to share their memories and compile information on where relatives, friends and acquaintances from this city had moved to: the USA, Canada, Israel, Australia or South Africa… Those familiar with the emigrant scene say that natives of Leipzig around the world are particularly attached to each other and have maintained intense contact for decades.

Eva Wechsberg's grandparents lived in Bernburg and so it was a priority for her during one of her visits in the 1990s to visit the Anhalt city with Dr. Hubert Lang, with whom she is particularly friendly and who spent a lot of time with her in Leipzig. The main destination was the Jewish cemetery. Eva wanted to go to the grave of her ancestors. Unfortunately, there was no longer a gravestone, but a map finally led them to find the spot, overgrown by nature, where Eva could commemorate her grandparents.

You could call Eva a small miracle — and not only due to her short stature. It's impossible to imagine that she will be a hundred in two years. My Jewish friends wish for "Mazel tov—to 120" on their birthdays. In Eva's case, all I can say is that I can't imagine why not.

Bernd-Lutz Lange,
Leipzig in July 2020

Afterword by Eva Wechsberg

As I sit here on my patio overlooking the Pacific Ocean, I feel incredibly fortunate and grateful to have lived such a long life surrounded by dear friends and a loving, ever-growing family. Reflecting on my early years, I lived in a beautiful city surrounded by a vibrant Jewish community numbering nearly fourteen thousand. After the war, there was no Jewish community in Leipzig. Some Jews had had the good luck to escape while others were taken to concentration camps, never to return. Knowing that in Leipzig there is once again, a small but active community of about thirteen hundred Jews, with the Head of Community Küf Kaufmann and under the religious care of Community Rabbi Zsolt Balla, indeed gives me hope.

From my first visit in 1996 to the most recent in 2019, I appreciate the continued efforts by the City of Leipzig, especially Mayor Burkhard Jung, Dr. Gabriele Goldfuß, Katja Roloff, and Dr. Sven Trautmann, to create each year, an even more meaningful experience for Jewish visitors. As the years go by, these visitors represent several generations of Jews, not only those who originated in Leipzig.

As I'm reminiscing, I'm thinking of some very special people, who for over more than 20 years have taken on various, meaningful projects. Dr. Andrea

Lorz has written several books about Jewish doctors in Leipzig, including the story of my father. Ellen Bertram has done major research and published two books carrying the name of *Menschen ohne Grabstein* (People without a Gravestone). The cover of the books depicts railroad tracks. It indicates but does not show the actual cattle cars that carried thousands of Jews to concentration camps. In looking through the first book, I found several friends who were murdered in those camps. Dr. Hubert Lang, who was my attorney for Wiedergutmachung and has become my dear friend wrote his thesis on Jewish lawyers, judges, and other jurists. The research took him back 150 years.

One of the most meaningful efforts has been the creation of thousands of "stumbling blocks" throughout Germany and even in some other European countries. These Stolpersteine are put in front of the homes where German Jews had lived until taken away to their deaths. My daughter Judy and I were present at the moving ceremony when a Stolperstein was laid in memory of Dr. Ludwig Frankenthal, the head of the Jewish hospital. I was touched when Dr. Lorz excused herself from a lovely luncheon, saying, "I now have to go and clean the Stolpersteine."

This book cannot be written without my comments about the amazing Leipzig Synagogal Choir who has brought Jewish liturgical synagogue music to Leipzig and other cities for more than 50 years. All the musicians are non-Jewish volunteers. In recent years, the conductor of the choir has been Ludwig Böhme, an outstanding musician, following in his father's footsteps. His father is the organist at the famous Thomaskirche. The last magnificent and meaningful event was the performance of the masterpiece Avodat Hakodesh by Ernest Bloch presented at the main train station (Hauptbahnhof) before one thousand people on June 30, 2019, which marked the end of the Jewish Week. Under Ludwig Böhme's masterful direction, it was an event I will never forget!

For those of you who know me, have heard me say, more than once, "History cannot be rewritten," and that is what I do believe. I am, however, grateful for the many efforts by the City of Leipzig and all those who continue their labor of love. It is because of those efforts and my frequent visits to what was once my hometown, I can say today, "Yes, it feels almost like coming home!"

Eva Wechsberg, born Abelsohn,
August 2020

Memorial event at the location where Leipzig Synagogue
stood in Gottschedstraße with the Minister President
of the Free State of Saxony, Michael Kretschmer,
November 9, 2018

List of illustrations

About the authors

Sven Trautmann

was born in Leipzig in 1989. He studied political science and African studies in Leipzig and Stellenbosch/South Africa. Since 2013 he has been organizing and supervising the Visitors' Programme for Former Jewish Leipzigers and their Descendants. He works as a Senior Project Manager at the Office for International Affairs of the City of Leipzig and is also responsible, among other things, for the city partnership between Leipzig and Herzliya/Israel. In 2020 he gained his Ph.D. with a thesis about international organizations.

Gabriele Goldfuß

was born in Nuremberg in 1963 and studied philosophy, sinology, and theology in Tübingen, Beijing, and Paris. She gained her Ph.D. in sinology, and from 1994 worked as a lecturer at the University of Leipzig. Since 2001, she has been Head of the Office for International Affairs of the City of Leipzig, where she is in charge of the European and international activities of the City of Leipzig, including partnerships with other cities and the Visitors' Programme for Former Jewish Leipzigers and their Descendants. She also supervises this network.

Andrea Lorz

was born in Altenburg in 1947. She studied history and education in Leipzig and gained her Ph.D. in Berlin. She worked as a scientific employee at various institutions in Leipzig and retired in 2012. Between 1996 and 2019 she published numerous publications about regional Jewish history, in particular about the work and achievements of Jewish doctors in Leipzig.

Jüdische Miniaturen Bd. 268
Deutsche Ausgabe

Eva Wechsberg
**Das Jahrhundertleben
einer jüdischen Leipzigerin**
88 Seiten, 23 Abbildungen
ISBN 978-3-95565-429-0, € 8,90